Book 3

MESSAGE ON THE STAMPS

Written by Jenny Phillips

Illustrations by Kessler Garrity
Cover Illustration by Brandon Dorman

Books in the Badger Hills Farm Series

The Secret Door

The Hidden Room

Message on the Stamps

Oak Tree Mystery

Clue in the Chimney

The Hills of Hirzel

TABLE OF CONTENTS

CHAPTER 1

TIMOTHY'S EYES POPPED OPEN, AND HE sat up in bed. The stars sprinkled in the dark sky told him that it was the middle of the night. Looking around the silent room, Timothy wondered what had woken him. *Was it a dream?* Timothy thought. *Was it a noise? Yes, I think I might've heard a noise. But what was it?*

He tiptoed to his window and looked out. A string of long gray clouds covered the moon, but the light from the nearby city bouncing off the clouds dimly lit the yard just enough for Timothy to make out shapes. He saw the huge piles of lumber and the big backhoe that had arrived yesterday to start building the barn.

Faintly, oh so faintly, Timothy was sure that he heard the crunching of gravel outside as if people were walking on the road. A quick glance at the clock by his bed showed it was after one in the morning. He carefully cracked the window and leaned his ear to the opening. There were whispered voices outside—he was sure of it! He backed away from the window a few steps, still trying to get oriented from being jolted awake. His mind spun. *What day is it? Oh yes, it's two days after Christmas. Nanna Rose and Papa George are here, and*

2

so is Zoey. Mom, Dad, and Nanna Bell had to go out of town suddenly.

Timothy tiptoed down the hall as fast as he could to the door of the guest room, where Nanna Rose and Papa George were sleeping, but then he hesitated. *Will they get mad if I wake them up? They are so nice, but I don't really know them very well. It feels weird to wake them up in the middle of the night.*

I know I heard something, so I have to wake them up. Taking a deep breath, he knocked on the door.

Timothy heard the floorboards creaking, and then the door opened slowly.

"Timothy? Is everything OK?" Papa George whispered with concern.

"I don't know. I heard people walking

around outside and whispering," Timothy replied.

"Let's go check it out," Papa George responded quickly as Nanna Rose joined them.

Papa George peered out the window in Timothy's room. "Hmmm, you were right," he whispered. "I see some people, maybe three or four of them, huddled around that big rock over there."

Timothy was worried. "I wonder who they are and what they're doing. What should we do?"

Placing a reassuring hand on Timothy's shoulder, Papa George spoke calmly. "It's OK, Timothy. I don't think we're in any danger. Don't turn on any lights, but carefully go downstairs and get that basket of pine cones in the family room."

Timothy obeyed promptly. He made his way to the family room even though he didn't understand what good pine cones would be. He returned a short time later with the basket.

Papa George quietly opened the window all the way. Without hesitation, he grabbed a pine cone from the basket and threw it out the window as hard as he could toward the shadowy figures. Then he threw another and another. Papa George turned to Timothy with a big smile on his face. "I haven't had this much fun in a long time! I'm not trying to hit them—just scare them off."

"Let's get out of here!" a voice called from outside, loud enough for Timothy to hear.

That didn't sound like an adult's voice, Timothy thought.

5

The sound of crunching gravel grew fainter and fainter as the people sped off.

Then all was still and quiet. With a little chuckle, Papa George said, "That was easy!"

Timothy smiled and hugged his grandfather. "Papa George, you are the best!"

"He is the best," agreed Nanna Rose, hugging both Timothy and her husband. Timothy felt an instant bond with these two wonderful people.

"Now, time for bed, Timothy," Nanna Rose said gently. "We're just down the hall if you need us again."

Timothy suddenly felt scared about staying in his room alone, but he couldn't tell them that. *I am twelve years old. What would they think of me if I told them I was scared?*

Nanna Rose studied Timothy's face and then turned to her husband. They smiled at each other and nodded.

"You know, I'm not feeling so tired anymore," Nanna Rose said. "I think I need to knit for a while first. Would you mind if I sat in one of these big, cozy chairs in your room? I know my knitting so well that I can even do it in the dark. It's quite relaxing, actually."

"Sure, no problem," Timothy said. Relieved, he slipped into his warm bed and turned toward the window, which Papa George had closed.

Papa George cleared his throat. "I'm not tired either. I'd like to go sit by the fireplace downstairs and read."

Nanna Rose soon returned with her

knitting and sat in one of the cozy chairs. The faint clicking of her knitting needles was so comforting that Timothy quickly drifted off to sleep.

CHAPTER 2

WHEN TIMOTHY AWOKE IN THE morning, he could tell by the bright sunshine pouring into the room that he had slept longer than normal.

Downstairs, he found Zoey putting on her boots and coat and Nanna Rose and Papa George all bundled up.

"Come on!" Zoey called to Timothy. "Papa George told me what happened last night. He went outside this morning to check on things, and he found something!"

"What did you find, Papa George?" Timothy asked as he took his jacket from the hook by the door and shoved his arms into the sleeves.

Papa George frowned. "I'll show you. It's on that rock where we saw the people last night."

Things sure seem much less scary in the day, Timothy thought as they walked out into the sunshine. A few quail strutted across the gravel path, and a bushy-tailed squirrel scampered up a tree. *It's hard to believe it snowed just a few days ago. It's not even that cold today.*

As they approached the large rock across from their home, Timothy and Zoey gasped. Red and black squiggly lines of spray paint covered the rock.

"It's so ugly!" Zoey said. "I loved this rock."

"Who would do this?" Timothy asked. "And why?"

"Those are good questions," Nanna Rose said. "Has anything like this happened before?"

"Never!" Timothy declared. "We haven't had any problems with trespassing."

"I was thinking of calling the police," Papa George stated, "but I doubt there is anything

they can do. It was probably just some teenagers. I doubt they'll come back."

Half an hour later, the family was eating breakfast by the blazing fire. Zoey and Timothy had made oatmeal with diced apples, cinnamon, and cream.

After breakfast, Zoey and Timothy ran out to the garage to see the chicks that had arrived the day after Christmas.

"Oh! They are so adorable," Zoey gushed as she looked into the large cage John had made. The fluffy little chicks chirped and chirped as they walked around the wood shavings and took occasional drinks from their water before darting back under the heating plate.

"They look so happy," Timothy commented. "I want to hold them, but Mom said we have to wait a few more days."

After doing chores and watching the tractor prepare the ground for the barn, Zoey and Timothy headed over to Mrs. Bastian's house to take care of Misty Toes and her foal.

"You're pretty quiet," Timothy said as they walked along the gravel road.

Zoey shrugged. "I'm just thinking about falling off Misty Toes."

Timothy frowned. He knew that Zoey was too scared to ride her beloved horse again, and it made him sad. "How is your head? Do the staples hurt when you sleep at night?"

"I sleep on my side, so I don't notice them. My head is sore, and I still have some big bruises on my hip and leg, but I'm OK."

Timothy tried to change the subject. "I'm glad that Mom and Dad will be home tonight, but I'll miss Nanna Bell. She said she might be gone for as long as a month. I hope her brother gets better. I guess his fall was worse than yours."

"Yeah, falling down a flight of stairs sounds terrible. I'm glad Nanna Bell is going to help take care of him while he recovers. It was nice of Mom and Dad to drive Nanna Bell so far to drop her off."

"I wonder what Mom and Dad will think about the graffiti on the rock," Timothy said.

That evening, after John and Lily had returned, dinner had been served, and the family had finished up their Bible study, Papa George explained about the graffiti.

"I was worried about this," John sighed. "I fear that more and more of this type of thing might happen. The stone walls around the property are old and tumbled down in many places. Fencing the property needs to be a top priority. There's just one problem, and you can all probably guess it."

Zoey nodded. "How to pay for it?"

"That's right," Lily responded. "John and I have already looked into pricing. To put up a chain-link fence around the entire farm will cost about two hundred fifty-five thousand dollars."

Papa George shook his head with a low whistle. "Wow, a quarter of a million dollars!"

"Yes," Lily agreed. "But what we would really like to have is a four-foot-high stone wall with a six-foot wrought iron fence on top. That way, it will protect the property and look really nice. We want Badger Hills Farm to be a beautiful place in the city for people to enjoy as they walk around it. The stone wall and iron fence would protect the farm, allow people to see the nature through the fence, and still be pretty. Also, wrought iron fences can last for over a hundred years! However, to build this kind of fence will cost just over a million dollars."

"A million dollars!" Timothy exclaimed. "We don't have that much money, do we?"

"No, we don't," Lily said. "We don't even have enough money to build a chain-link fence."

"A perimeter fence is not the only fence we'll need," John declared. "Lily and I have been talking, and we don't think we can build the campground without enclosing it with a fence. We just don't think it's a good idea to have people wandering all around the property. But there is no money for that fence either," John explained.

"So what are we going to do?" Zoey asked.

Rubbing his chin, John looked into the fire. "I don't know."

Timothy noticed the stamp collection book sitting on the shelf. "What about the stamp collection?" he asked. "Some of those stamps could be worth a fortune."

John straightened in his chair. "Hmmm. I forgot about the stamps with all the busyness of Christmas and driving Nanna Bell to take care of her brother. But I did flip through it, and the stamps look very old. Some could be quite valuable. I'm not sure how to find out, though."

"Maybe we could ask Mrs. Sanchez," Lily offered. "She was talking about auctions for antique art and furniture. Maybe there are auctions for stamps."

"Great idea!" John declared. "We should visit her tomorrow."

"Can we look at the stamps right now?" Timothy asked.

John shook his head. "Time for bed. But we can look at them right after breakfast tomorrow."

CHAPTER 3

THE WIND WAS GUSTING FURIOUSLY THE next morning. Timothy looked out his window before heading downstairs. It seemed the wind had swept the sky completely clean; a golden sun was rising in a cloudless sky.

Nanna Rose and Papa George had been up for a while making breakfast. Timothy was shocked when he walked into the kitchen and looked at the breakfast table. White cloth napkins were folded into swans. There were plates with strawberries beautifully carved into roses, heart-shaped fried eggs sprinkled with fresh herbs, and a large loaf of cinnamon twist bread shaped into a star and sprinkled with powdered sugar.

"What is all this?" Timothy exclaimed.

Zoey grinned as she sat down at the table. "Don't you remember, Timothy? Papa George was a professional chef at a fancy restaurant before he retired."

"This is amazing!" Timothy marveled.

After breakfast, everyone gathered in the family room. John set up the long folding table in front of the flickering flames waving merrily in the fireplace. Everyone gathered around John as he set the stamp collection book on the table and opened it up.

"Oh, those stamps do look old," Timothy commented. "How many are there?"

"There are one hundred two stamps total," John said.

·"I can try looking up their value," Lily offered, pulling out her phone. "Of course, there are things to consider that we don't know much about, like the condition of the stamp. But this will give us an idea. Which one should we start with, Zoey?"

"Let's do the green one-cent stamp with Benjamin Franklin on it," Zoey replied, pointing to it.

Excitedly, Lily researched on her phone and then declared, "It's worth around three hundred dollars. Although, if it is in great condition and was never used, it could be worth up to eleven thousand dollars!"

"It was used," John said. "As I looked

through the stamps, I noticed that all but four have postmarks on them."

A roller coaster of emotions carried Timothy on quite the exciting ride. *Will one of these stamps be worth a lot of money?* he wondered.

"Which one should we research next?" Lily asked Timothy.

"Let's do this two-cent red one with George Washington on it," Timothy said.

After researching the price, Lily looked up from her phone. "Four hundred fifty-nine dollars!" she declared.

"Have you heard of the Inverted Jenny stamp?" Nanna Rose asked. "It was issued over one hundred years ago and had an airplane called the 'Jenny' in the middle of it. A sheet of one hundred stamps was accidentally printed with the airplane upside down, and now those stamps are worth quite a bit."

Lily had been typing on her phone, and now she gasped. "Inverted Jennys can sell for a million dollars!"

"Are there any Inverted Jennys in the album?" Timothy asked.

"I don't remember all the stamps," John said. "I'll look through them more carefully."

He started turning the pages. Suddenly, a bell dinged, and everyone jumped a little.

Over by the door, Sammy stood next to a little bell, looking at everyone expectantly.

"He used the bell we put by the door," Timothy said. "That means he wants to be let outside. Mrs. Minks has been training him on that. It seems to be working!"

Smiling, Timothy went to the door. "Good job, Sammy!"

As the door opened, a strong gust of wind pushed its way into the room, wildly ruffling the pages of the stamp collection book. As if in slow motion, Timothy watched three stamps fly out of the book. One stamp landed on the floor, but the other two twirled in the air and flew right over the fireplace grill into the fire.

"No!" Timothy cried.

"Oh! The stamps! The stamps!" cried Zoey.

Everyone watched helplessly as the fire engulfed the two stamps.

"What if one of those was an Inverted Jenny?" Zoey cried suddenly. She put her hands on her hips and turned to Timothy.

"Oh! If only you had been more careful about opening the door!"

Tears stung Timothy's eyes. He turned and dashed out of the room, up the stairs, and down the hallway. In his room, he flopped facedown on his bed and cried. *Zoey is so mad at me. What if everyone else is mad at me too? I didn't mean to. But it is my fault. I should've thought more carefully before I opened the door.*

A few minutes later, someone knocked softly on Timothy's door. "Can I come in?" Lily asked.

"I guess," he replied softly.

Having decided that he was ready for the day to be over, Timothy had put his pajamas back on and tucked himself into bed.

Lily knelt next to the bed and stroked

28

his hair. "I know how you must be feeling, Timothy, but it was an honest mistake. No one is mad at you."

"Zoey is," Timothy responded.

"Not anymore. She feels bad that she said anything."

As she continued to stroke Timothy's hair, Lily told him about the time she accidentally flooded her bathroom when she was a child. The water had soaked through the bathroom floor and started pouring through the ceiling into her father's office below. The water not only ruined the ceiling, but it also dripped right onto her father's head.

As Timothy listened, he couldn't help smiling and thinking how nice it was to feel the concern of a mother.

"Thank you, Mom," he said, getting out of bed and sitting next to Lily.

"Now," Lily said, "Papa George is packing a picnic basket. I can only imagine all the amazing food he is putting in it. Zoey is

waiting for you downstairs, very anxious to tell you how sorry she is for getting mad. This is the warmest day we've had in weeks. I thought I could work on looking up the value of the stamps, which will take me hours, while you and Zoey look for Hannah's white oak tree. Maybe you can add to the map you're creating as you go. How can you do that if you're in your pajamas?"

Timothy smiled widely. "I can be out of my pajamas and into my clothes in less than two minutes!"

"Excellent!" Lily said as she stood up. "I'll see you downstairs in two minutes!"

CHAPTER 4

AFTER WATCHING THE BACKHOE GRADING the land for the barn, Timothy and Zoey set out to explore Badger Hills Farm, something they had been wanting to get back to since Zoey hurt her ankle before Christmas.

Timothy wore a backpack that contained mittens and hats in case it got colder, along with a notebook, pencils, and water bottles. Zoey carried the picnic basket. With a twinkle in his eye, Papa George had handed the basket to the kids and said, "Don't peek into it until you are ready to eat."

As they walked down the gravel road and then veered off into the forest, Timothy breathed in the beauty around him. Since starting his painting lessons and being introduced to books with beautiful descriptions, Timothy saw the world around him differently. Things he never would have noticed before jumped out at him, such as the ferns lining the little stream and swaying like a rolling ocean in the breeze, the pattern of light and shadows on the forest floor, and the joyful twittering of birds.

"We have so much to explore and map," Zoey stated. "What should we do first?"

"Well, I'm really interested to know about

the streams: how many there are and where they stop and start," Timothy said, pulling out a notebook and pencil. "I'll map as we walk. We just have to go very slowly."

The two continued talking as they followed a stream through the trees.

"I almost wish we had stayed to watch Lily look up the values of all the stamps. I can't wait to see what she finds," Zoey said.

"I know," Timothy agreed. "But I'm not sure I could've waited while she looked up the value of a hundred stamps!"

A robin floated past the children, and a slight breeze rippled the golden grass. Timothy looked up into the bright blue sky and took in a deep breath. *What an amazing day!*

After following the stream for an hour, they discovered that it entered the property through a large pipe and left the property through another.

"Let's look for Hannah's white oak tree now," Zoey suggested. "There are so many large oak trees on the property. How will we know which one it is?"

"Remember the map in the hidden room?" Timothy asked. "It showed that Hannah's white oak tree is near the place where one of the other streams forks into two. Let's look for that."

"Oh yeah! And the map said there is an abandoned badger den right at that same fork in the stream. It was labeled in red, which means it's important somehow."

Over the rolling hills and through small groves they went, laughing and talking. The world seemed calm and quiet and slow moving, and Timothy thought it was nice not to feel rushed. They watched a chipmunk and collected a few interesting rocks. Then they tried to memorize different bird songs so that they could identify the birds just by the sounds.

"There will be even more birds in the spring and summer," Zoey commented. "And I can't wait to see what it's like here when all the plants and trees come back to life."

Timothy nodded his agreement. Then he shaded his eyes with his hand and pointed. "Look! It's a fork in the stream! And I see a little mound by it. I bet it's the abandoned badger den."

The children ran toward the mound and found that it was indeed a badger's den, but they weren't sure it was abandoned.

"Look! There are animal tracks all around here, and they even go right into the den," Zoey said.

"Let's not get too close," Timothy said, remembering his encounter with the badger in the kitchen the day he had found the secret door.

"You know," Zoey wondered aloud as Timothy drew in his notebook, "it was because of a badger that you found the secret door. That's pretty neat, considering this land is called Badger Hills Farm."

"That is neat!" Timothy agreed. "I wonder if that den was abandoned at one point but now maybe badgers live in it again. Or maybe another animal lives in it."

"We should take pictures of the footprints next time and identify them," Timothy said, turning his gaze to the right. "Oh, look! That must be Hannah's white oak tree. It's the biggest oak tree I've seen on the farm, and it is right where the map in the hidden room says it should be."

Zoey clapped her hands and began running. "Let's go check it out!"

Breathing heavily, they arrived at the tree and stood under it in awe.

Zoey touched the rough bark and traced her fingers along a huge knob growing in the tree.

As Timothy looked up, he noted how thick the trunk was and how beautifully the branches curved and arched as they reached in every direction. "Wow! This tree is absolutely amazing!"

"I know," Zoey exclaimed. She sat down against the tree and leaned back with a sigh. Then she peeked into the picnic basket next to her. "You know what else is amazing? This picnic lunch. Let's eat!"

CHAPTER 5

TIMOTHY POPPED THE LAST BITE OF bacon-wrapped pickle into his mouth and then slowly ate the flaky pine-nut pastry that was shaped like a pine cone.

"Wow, that was an amazing lunch! It was so nice of Papa George to make it," Zoey exclaimed as she stood up. "Let's explore around the tree. Maybe we can find out why it's an important item marked in red on the big map in the hidden room."

While Zoey walked slowly around the tree several times, Timothy sketched on his map.

"Nothing!" Zoey pronounced. "It's an incredible tree, but I don't see anything important about it." She stood looking at the wide trunk. "Wait! Something is carved here. It's a heart."

"Does it have letters on it?" Timothy asked, coming over to investigate.

"Yes!" Zoey moved her face closer to the tree. "I think I see 'H + A' carved inside the heart. Oh! 'H' could be for Hannah, but who is 'A' for?"

"We should check the Roach family's photo album that Dad got from the hidden room," suggested Timothy.

"Yes!" Zoey cried. "I forgot about that. I

want to see what Hannah looks like, and maybe we'll find out who the 'A' stands for."

"But why is the tree important?" Timothy asked.

"Good question," Zoey said. "I have so many questions. Simon's note said that all the items from the hidden room hold clues, except the Bible. I've looked all over my ceramic oak tree, and I haven't found any clues on it."

"Oh, does it look like this tree?"

Zoey thought for a second. "Yes, it does, actually!"

Thick clouds had moved in to cover the sun, and a cool breeze picked up.

Timothy put his notebook and pencil in the backpack and pulled out the mittens and hats, handing a set to Zoey and putting a set on himself. "Wait a minute. Clues! You're right! That means the stamps in the stamp collection book must hold clues too."

Zoey's eyes grew wide. "Ooooh!"

"So maybe we shouldn't sell the stamps because we will need them as clues for something else," Timothy said.

"Let's go home and examine the stamps more closely," Zoey suggested.

"Agreed," Timothy said as they began walking. He frowned, thinking of the two stamps that had flown into the fireplace. *What if those stamps had clues on them?*

When the kids reached the deer enclosure, they opened the fence and continued following the stream. Through the trees, Timothy saw a group of deer standing as still as statues. They watched Timothy and Zoey intently before bounding away.

After a few more minutes, Zoey stopped walking. "Listen," she whispered. "I hear voices."

"Me too," Timothy replied in a low voice.

Then Timothy and Zoey saw a group of teenage boys by one of the gates of the deer enclosure.

"They are spray-painting it!" Zoey cried, so loudly that the teenagers spun around and saw her.

"Let's get out of here!" one of the boys yelled.

Timothy watched as the teenagers threw the hoods of their sweatshirts over their heads and dashed out of the gate, leaving it wide open.

Even from that distance, Timothy could see that the gate was crisscrossed with green and yellow paint.

"Oh no," he moaned. "Come on! Let's go shut the gate and then go tell Mom and Dad."

They reached the house and burst through the door, startling John and Lily. Timothy and Zoey both started talking at once, their words flying around the room in a jumbled mess.

"Whoa!" John laughed. "I'm hearing something about Hannah's white oak tree, a heart, clues on the stamps, teenagers, spray paint, and even bacon-wrapped pickles. Why don't you slow down and start again from the beginning?"

Zoey and Timothy laughed too, and Timothy told them about their adventures, frowning when he got to the part about the teenagers and the spray paint.

John shook his head. "I don't like that news at all. Maybe we need to notify the police about the trespassing."

"Maybe we should put up cameras," Lily suggested. "Except it would take a lot of cameras to cover the entire farm."

Mrs. Minks arrived for dog obedience classes, so the family decided to think about what should be done to stop the trespassers from spray-painting the farm. With the unsolved problem still in their heads, the one-hour lesson felt longer than normal, but it was still fun.

"Sammy is really improving," Mrs. Minks said as she prepared to leave. "He's a wonderful dog!"

"Yes, he is!" Timothy agreed. "Thank you so much for your lessons, Mrs. Minks."

"You know," Mrs. Minks said, "you have thanked me sincerely after every lesson. Not many boys do that."

Timothy blushed. "Oh, well—"

"It's a good trait," Mrs. Minks said. "A really good trait. Do you know who Aesop is?"

"Of course!" Timothy smiled. "We did a homeschool lesson on him recently."

"Well, Aesop said, 'Gratitude is the sign of noble souls.' If you think about it, you will find so many people that you can express gratitude to every day. In fact, I made a goal recently to express gratitude for something to every member of my family every day, even my dogs. It's really brought me a lot of joy."

Timothy smiled and waved as Mrs. Minks left. He liked the thought of having a noble soul, and Mrs. Minks's kind words made him want to be even more noble. *I think I'll try thanking every person in my family for something every day too—even Sammy.*

Timothy knelt down by Sammy and patted his back. "Thank you, Sammy, for trying so hard during your obedience lessons. You're doing great!"

As if he understood, Sammy gave a little bark and then licked Timothy's hand.

Timothy then found Papa George and thanked him for all the amazing food he made that day. Next, he thanked Nanna Rose for sitting with him and knitting while he went back to sleep.

50

Looking for Mom and Dad, Timothy went into the family room. There, he found the stamp book sitting on the table with a notebook beside it.

Timothy slid into a chair and studied Lily's handwriting on the open page of the notebook. She had numbered the lines one to one hundred, and there was a dollar amount by each number. *Ah, this is her research on the value of the stamps*, Timothy thought. The amounts ranged anywhere from thirty dollars to six hundred fifty dollars. At the bottom of the page it said, "Total: $10,653."

"That's a lot of money," Timothy said aloud, "but not enough for a fence."

"That's right!" Lily declared as she, John, and Zoey came into the room. "But Zoey just

51

reminded us about Simon's note and how it said that each item had clues." She handed Timothy a big magnifying glass. "Do you want to investigate the stamps for us, Timothy?"

"Sure!" Timothy opened the stamp collection book to the first page.

CHAPTER 6

C AREFULLY, TIMOTHY INSPECTED EACH of the stamps. *It's pretty fun using the magnifying glass*, he thought.

But by the time he got halfway through the stamps, he had not seen anything, and his eyes were getting really tired. "Would you like a turn?" he asked Zoey.

Excitedly, Zoey took the magnifying glass and stamp collection and began searching.

After the last stamp, she set the magnifying

glass down with a disappointed sigh.
"Nothing!"

"Well, I called Mrs. Sanchez earlier today,"
Lily began, "and she said her brother-in-law
is actually a stamp and art dealer. She's going
to ask when he could come over to tell us how
much the stamps are worth."

"But maybe we shouldn't sell the stamps

54

yet in case there are clues that we find later," Timothy said.

John nodded. "I agree. But let's find out how much they are worth in the meantime."

Lily went over to the couch. "I twisted my back a little chopping wood this morning. I'm going to lie down and rest my back."

"Back!" Timothy cried suddenly. "Back!"

"What are you saying, Timothy?" Zoey asked.

"The backs of the stamps," he explained. "Let's look on the backs of the stamps! Can I, Dad?"

"Yes, but very carefully."

Nanna Rose and Papa George joined them.

"I've been reading a lot about stamps since last night," said Nanna Rose. "I learned that you shouldn't touch old stamps with your hands. That's because your hands have oils on them and even some dirt you might not see."

"We can use tweezers," John stated.

With a shake of her head, Nanna Rose said, "No, tweezers could damage the stamps, too, because they are sharp. You need to use stamp tongs."

"Stamp tongs?" Timothy asked curiously. "What are stamp tongs?"

"Well," explained Nanna Rose, "they are very much like tweezers, but they are flat on the ends instead of sharp and pointy."

"I have an idea," Lily said, sitting up on the couch. "Why don't we make some stamp tongs?"

"How would we do that?" Zoey asked.

"We could melt a little wax and dip the ends of the tweezers in it and then let it dry. That way the tweezers won't be sharp."

"Our daughter is brilliant," Papa George said to Nanna Rose with a grin.

Soon Timothy and Zoey were huddled around a candle, watching as Lily dipped the tip of the tweezers into melted wax and then held it up to dry.

"It looks great!" Lily declared. "Zoey, would you like to turn over the first stamp?"

"Sure!" Zoey sang, taking the tweezers, gently pulling out the first stamp from the book and turning it over.

Everyone gasped at the same time when they saw a word on the back of the stamp: "figure."

"'Figure'?" Zoey said. "What does that mean?"

"Turn over the next stamp," Timothy urged.

Zoey's hands were shaking with excitement, so she took a few deep breaths and then slowly pulled out and turned over the next stamp. Everyone gasped again. There was another word.

"'Out,'" Zoey shared. "The two words together say, 'Figure out.' Figure what out?"

"Turn over the next stamp," Timothy urged again.

"I can't! My hands are shaking too much now. This is so exciting!" Zoey giggled.

Nanna Rose spoke up. "Too bad there are words written on the back. I read that if there is writing on a stamp, it is worth less money."

"Yes, but the clues may lead us to something more valuable than all these stamps together," Lily explained.

Handing the tweezers to Timothy, Zoey said, "Here, you do it!"

Timothy took the tweezers and carefully turned the stamps over in the order they had been put in the stamp book, row by row. Some of the words were hard to read.

When Timothy got to a few stamps in a row that had no writing on them, they all stopped and read the words that Timothy had turned over:

Figure out the order,
And you will be surprised
To find a sentence that declares
Where the treasure hides.

"I knew it!" Zoey said, taking a little leap into the air. "I knew it! There is a valuable treasure somewhere in this house!"

Lily started laughing and hugged Timothy. Nanna Rose was clapping her hands.

"Wait!" John called out above all the noise. "'Figure out the order'? What does that mean?"

It suddenly got very quiet. No one knew what "figure out the order" meant.

"Let's turn over the rest of the stamps and see if there are more clues," Lily encouraged.

"Great idea," Timothy replied as he picked up the tweezers. The backs of the next two stamps were also blank. But the stamp after that had a letter written on it. It was a lowercase "r."

The next two stamps had letters on them as well.

"Letters!" Zoey exclaimed. "I wish there were more words instead of letters."

"Me too, Zoey," Lily said. "But the letters mean something. We just have to figure out the puzzle Simon left us."

Timothy turned over the rest of the stamps, and these are the letters that they found:

e r T a s t p t a t c i s i n h e r h s s e o e m

Timothy counted them. "Twenty-five letters. I'm guessing we need to put those letters in order to create a sentence."

"Only one of them is uppercase," Papa George noted. "That must be the beginning of the sentence that we are supposed to decode."

"I have an idea," Lily said as she ran out of

the room. Soon she came back with a board game. "Letter tiles!" she explained.

From the game, Lily took out letter tiles to match the letters that they had found on the stamps. "We can use these to try arranging the sentence so we don't ruin the stamps moving them around."

"Oh, let me try!" Nanna Rose cried. "I'm the queen of word games."

Everyone laughed and made room for Nanna Rose, who sat down in front of the letter tiles.

After trying for over twenty minutes, Nanna Rose pushed back her chair. "Ah! I give up. Someone else try."

And try they did! For hours, they arranged letters into words, trying to make the words into a sentence that made sense. They each took turns and cheered each other on. Papa George brought in dinner on trays.

Finally, the grandfather clock in the hallway struck eleven o'clock.

"Let's call it a night!" Lily insisted.

CHAPTER 7

For THREE DAYS IT RAINED OFF AND ON, leaving Badger Hills Farm spotted with puddles and patches of mud. Little rivulets of water ran down the hills into the streams, and gray skies lay like a heavy cloak over the farm.

Since it was still Christmas break, Timothy and Zoey had a lot of extra time to try unscrambling the letters to solve the message on the stamps. But try as they might, they couldn't come up with any combination of words that made much sense. John, Lily, Nanna Rose, and Papa George all tried without success. Diego and Jessica came over for hours on end and tried. Mrs. Minks insisted on trying, as did Mrs. Bastian, but none of them could make any sense of the letters.

Mrs. Sanchez's brother-in-law came over and studied the stamps for hours. His name was Mr. Garcia. He had a jolly, booming voice and the longest mustache Timothy had ever seen.

"The collection is probably worth around nine thousand dollars," Mr. Garcia declared. "But I will personally buy it from you right now for ten thousand dollars."

John thanked Mr. Garcia for his help but said he wanted to think about it for a while.

Zoey and Timothy tried once more to find

the message. "I officially give up," Zoey said. "This puzzle will never be solved. This rain has forced us inside for days, and all we've done is try to solve this puzzle. It's no use."

Timothy stood up. "I know what you mean.

I wish we could've been exploring the farm instead."

"Yes, I can't wait to go back to Hannah's white oak tree," Zoey replied.

"And I also want to take pictures of any fresh animal prints by the badger's den so we can try to identify the animal that may be living there."

Zoey went to the window. "The clouds have cleared up now—finally! But there's not enough light left in the day to venture out."

"And church is tomorrow, so it's not a day to explore," Timothy remarked.

"And the day after that is Monday, and we start homeschool again. Christmas break will be officially over." Zoey sighed softly. She loved learning but was a little sorry that the break was over too.

"One good thing about the weather is that it probably kept those teenagers away from our land," Timothy said.

Zoey nodded. "That's true! Well, we can keep exploring after school next week if there's good weather."

Monday came dancing in clear and bright. Above the rosy, gold tints of the dawn, a stream of blue sky smiled over the farm and set Timothy's heart to singing.

In the middle of breakfast in the family room, Timothy dropped his fork. "I think I know why we can't make a sentence with the stamps." He took a deep breath before continuing. "I bet the two stamps that flew in the fire had letters on them, and without those letters, we can't figure it out."

Lily stood up and walked over to Timothy. She put her hands on his shoulders. "Don't worry, Timothy. It was an accident. Those stamps might not have even had letters on them."

"But they must have. I just know it. Everyone has tried to make words from the letters with no success," Timothy said sadly.

Looking down at her phone, Lily cocked her head. "Hmmm. I just got a really interesting text message from Mrs. Bastian. Let me read it to you: 'Hello! As you know, I've been out of town the past couple of days. I brought the Bible Zoey gave me, thinking I might read some of it. Something handwritten in the Bible made me think of a way that we could possibly decode the message on the stamps. I'll be home the day after tomorrow. Would you mind if I waited until then to tell you what I am thinking? I'd really like to be there with you and see if my idea actually works.'"

"Tell her to tell us right now!" Timothy urged.

With a shake of her head, Lily started typing a message back on her phone. "You know that's not polite, Timothy. She really wants to be here. I know it's hard to wait for two days, but the sunny weather today will probably dry up all the mud and puddles on the farm, and then tomorrow you and Zoey can go explore and map more of Badger Hills Farm after you finish your schoolwork."

A rumble outside brought everyone to the window.

"Look at all those trucks!" Timothy called, watching a stream of construction vehicles coming up the gravel road.

"They are going to asphalt the road," Zoey said. "Will they finish before Mrs. Bastian gets home?"

"I don't think so," Lily said. "It will take them a couple of days to lay the asphalt, and then it will take a few more days for it to dry fully. But your dad can get Mrs. Bastian in the golf cart, using the trails."

"Sounds fun!" Timothy smiled.

Taking advantage of the good weather, Timothy and Zoey did a lot of their schoolwork on the back patio that day.

They took a break and talked while lying in their hammocks.

"You know what I am so scared of?" Zoey started.

"What?"

"That those teenagers are going to paint graffiti on places like Hannah's white oak tree."

"I know," Timothy replied. "I can't wait to put a fence around this property. Man, I hope that Mrs. Bastian's idea really works."

"Me too. But what if it doesn't lead to a valuable treasure? We really need to find a way to get the money for a fence."

"Well," Timothy said, sitting up. "The stamps are not the only item from the hidden room that has clues."

"That's right!" Zoey agreed, turning to Timothy. "Maybe one of the other items will lead to something valuable."

They looked at each other and smiled.

"Are you thinking what I'm thinking?" Timothy asked.

"Yes!" Zoey burst out. "Let's go check the other items."

Laughing and whooping, they ran into the house. Using her new phone watch, Zoey texted Nanna Bell and got permission to inspect her clock.

"OK! Let's press and pull and tap every part of the clock that we can," Timothy told Zoey. "Maybe there is a secret compartment in it."

They didn't find anything.

"Well, let's go look at your oak tree figurine," Timothy suggested.

Zoey shook her head. "No, I've already done that a hundred times. There's nothing that I can see. Even when I shake it, it doesn't make any sound. It's so heavy that I don't think it's hollow."

"That's the way I feel about the map in my room," Timothy said. "There are no clues at all other than the title of the map: 'lezrih.' That doesn't mean anything to me."

"Wait!" Zoey cried, grabbing a paper and pencil from Nanna Bell's desk. "How do you spell that?"

Timothy spelled "lezrih" slowly while Zoey wrote it down. Then she chewed her pencil for a moment before scribbling on the paper. She held it up for Timothy to see. "Look at this. The word 'lezrih' spelled backward is 'hirzel.' Do you think that 'hirzel' is the name of a real place?"

"Let's find out," Timothy said.

Timothy and Zoey dashed down the hallway to John's office. After getting his permission to research on the computer, Timothy searched for "hirzel" on the internet. He found that Hirzel was the name of a village in Switzerland.

Zoey pressed her hands together and brought them to her chin in excitement. "Oh! Do you think that this map is of Hirzel?"

Timothy was reading about the village on the internet. He gasped. "Zoey, Hirzel is where Johanna Spyri was born. The books that Lily got from the hidden room—they are original books by Johanna Spyri."

CHAPTER 8

U NBELIEVABLE," LILY SAID FOR ABOUT the tenth time. "There has got to be some connection between Timothy's map and the book set by Johanna Spyri."

"Let's go to Hirzel!" Zoey burst out, her eyes shining.

Timothy laughed. "I agree!"

"But I don't think it would really help to go there right now," John reasoned. "There are no 'X marks the spot' type things on the map.

We wouldn't know what to do with the map if we went there."

"Yeah, there are some things that look like rivers, and there are some hills and some boxes here and there, but that's all. There are no roads or labels or anything," Timothy said.

"So many mysteries!" Nanna Rose exclaimed. "Simon and his family were really quite the interesting people to create all this."

"It's so fun," Zoey declared.

"Yes, it is," Lily agreed. "I don't think there is anything more we can find out about Timothy's map right now. There could be a clue in the Johanna Spyri books, but I can't read them because they're in German. I've actually always wanted to learn German, so I'm going to start an online program, but I imagine it will take years to learn it well enough to read these books."

"With all the excitement about the map, we forgot to study the vase and photo album from the hidden room," Timothy remarked. "Can we look at your vase, Lily?"

"Of course! I'll go get it."

The children didn't discover any messages or clues on the vase, but they did admire the little cottage and nature scene painted on it.

"Simon's note said that each item except the Bible had clues, so this vase does hold a clue," Zoey reminded everyone. "We just don't know what it is yet."

Timothy and Zoey enjoyed the photo album as well. They had flipped through the pages before, but now they spent over half an hour studying the photos. Afterward, it felt like they knew Simon and his family even better. This is what Simon's family looked like.

Simon and Tabitha's Wedding

Simon Tabitha and Hannah

Simon
Tabitha
Hannah
and
baby Caleb

Hannah
age 8
Caleb
age 4

There were several more spreads in the album that showed the children as they were growing up on the farm.

"Well!" said Timothy as he closed the book and stood up. "That was great to see, but we should probably get back to our schoolwork. Mom wants us to finish up math and language arts before you go get the staples taken out of your head and I go to art lessons with Mrs. Sanchez."

"Let's watch the workers outside making the asphalt road first," Zoey suggested.

"Great idea. I also want to watch the workers who are framing the barn," Timothy added. "There's a lot going on right now at Badger Hills Farm!"

The next day dawned clear and bright again. The puddles were gone, and the mud had dried. After lunch, Timothy and Zoey grabbed their jackets and headed out to explore Badger Hills Farm. They spent hours mapping the grounds. In the late afternoon, a breeze picked up, and long strings of gray clouds rolled in.

At the badger's den, they found fresh animal tracks. With the phone borrowed from Lily, Zoey took pictures of the tracks.

The last spot they visited was Hannah's white oak tree. Once again, Zoey explored all around the tree and found no clues. It was a great place to sit and talk, though. They leaned against the wide trunk and gazed out over the farm as they chatted.

Early in the evening when they returned

to the house, they found that John and Lily had already left to take Nanna Rose and Papa George out to eat. Timothy and Zoey were staying home by themselves. Dusk was starting to fall upon the farm when Zoey came flying into the room.

"The phone! Lily's phone! I can't find it anywhere."

"Where is the last place you remember having it?" Timothy inquired.

After a moment of thought, Zoey replied, "I know I had it at Hannah's white oak tree because I took a bunch of pictures of the tree. But then I set it down beside me as we talked. Oh, I think I left it there."

Zoey looked out the window. "I think we have enough time left to go get it before it gets dark. It looks like it could rain tonight."

Timothy nodded. "But we should call Mom and Dad and tell them where we are going."

"Our phone watches are dead, remember?" Zoey said. "I'm afraid if we wait a few minutes for them to charge, it will be too dark to go out."

Timothy put his hands on his hips. "I think we should just charge up our watches enough to call Mom and Dad. We're not supposed to leave the house after dark."

"I know, but this is different. If we wait, it's going to be dark, and then it could rain, and the phone would be ruined. And if we just go now, well . . . we don't have to tell them that I forgot the phone. We can get there and back in less than half an hour. It's not a big deal.

Please, Timothy," Zoey pleaded.

Timothy sighed. "All right, but let's hurry. I'll grab some flashlights, just in case," he suggested.

They rushed out the door, leaving so quickly they didn't realize they hadn't completely shut the door behind them. The breeze soon pushed it wide open.

Across the farm they dashed, jumping over little streams and weaving through the trees.

When they were getting close to the tree, they heard noises—people talking and laughing.

Timothy grabbed Zoey and pulled her behind a bush.

In the shadowy dusk, Timothy was able to make out a group of people, and it didn't take long to see that it was the teenagers and that they were spray-painting a large rock.

Looking around on the ground, Timothy found a few pine cones and chucked them over by the boys. Then, still hidden behind the bush, he called out in a deep voice, "Who trespasses on this property?"

In a panic, the teenagers ran away.

"Come on!" urged Timothy. "Let's go get the phone and go home. I don't like being out here when it's getting dark."

With relief, they found the phone sitting at the base of the tree, where Zoey had left it. After snatching it up, they started back.

"We shouldn't run," Zoey said. "There's not enough light to see well, and we could trip or twist an ankle."

Timothy flipped on a flashlight and handed another one to Zoey. "I agree, but this will help."

Seeing movement out of the corner of his eye, Timothy flashed his light over to the left. The light fell on a pair of green eyes shining in the dark.

"Oh no," Timothy breathed.

"I see it," whispered Zoey, shining her light in the same direction. The eyes disappeared behind a bush. "I didn't get a good look, but I think it's a badger. It may be going to the den."

Remembering the growling and snarling badger that he had found in the kitchen, Timothy turned around and started running.

"Wait!" Zoey yelled. "That's the wrong way!"

"We'll take the long way around! Come on!" Timothy called.

Zoey was out of breath by the time she caught up to Timothy and grabbed his hand, forcing him to stop running.

Before Zoey could say anything to Timothy, they heard a voice call out.

"Help! Help me, please!"

CHAPTER 9

TIMOTHY QUICKLY FORGOT THE GLOWING green eyes as the distressed voice echoed through the trees.

Cautiously, they followed the voice, which led them to a group of tall bushes. Suddenly, the beam of a flashlight fell on a teenage boy wearing a black sweatshirt and black sweatpants.

The boy abruptly stopped yelling. "Oh please, help me. I'm trapped," he said.

Timothy quickly observed the situation. The boy's long hair was badly tangled in the bushes, trapping him there.

"Wait, you're one of the boys spray-painting our farm," Zoey said with narrowed eyes.

"Yes, I am, but I'm sorry—really. I didn't actually do any of the spray-painting myself. When we ran off, it was pretty dark, and I didn't realize these bushes were so close together. My hair is tangled up in the branches so badly that I can't get out."

Timothy saw that there were several deep scratches on the boy's face and that they were bleeding.

"Why didn't the other boys wait for you?" Zoey asked.

A hardened look came into the boy's eyes, and he looked away. "They left me here because they didn't want to get caught."

Zoey and Timothy went off several feet, put their heads together, and whispered.

"Let's get him out," Zoey suggested.

"But what if he hurts us when he gets out?" Timothy objected.

"I have Lily's phone," Zoey exclaimed, holding it up. "Let's call Mom and Dad."

She tapped on the screen several times but then sighed softly. "It's dead."

"Please, help me!" the boy called again. "This bush is practically tearing my hair out every time I move."

"I don't think he'll hurt us," Zoey decided.

"OK," Timothy agreed.

Timothy held the flashlight as Zoey worked on the boy's hair. After a while Timothy's arms ached from holding up the light, and he shivered. Dusk had been swallowed up by the night, and it was cold.

An owl swooped across the sky above them with a soft swooshing sound and a lonely "whoo-whoo."

"Hurry, Zoey!" Timothy begged.

"I'm going as fast as I can. I can't believe how tangled his hair is. He must have been thrashing around, getting it more and more tangled. If I had scissors, I could cut it off."

After thirty minutes of trying, Zoey finally sighed and dropped her hands. "I just can't get it. We need to go home and get scissors. Besides, Mom and Dad are probably home by now," Zoey continued, "and they are likely worried sick about us."

The boy groaned. "Oh no, don't bring your parents."

"They will help. They're very nice," Timothy insisted.

"Yeah, right! They are going to be very nice to the boy who has been trespassing on their farm. I'll be in so much trouble. Listen, please just try a little more. If you can get me out, I promise I won't ever come on your farm again."

With a sigh, Zoey tried again. After ten more minutes, she gave up. "It's no use. Really. You are not getting out of here without scissors."

Zoey turned to Timothy. "I don't think it's safe for just one of us to wait here. Let's both go together to get scissors."

"OK," Timothy agreed. "But if Mom and Dad are not back from dinner, we are plugging in the phone and calling Dad before we come back. We should have let him know before we came out here."

Zoey climbed out of the bushes. "Let's hurry then!"

"Yeah, get going, you two!" the boy said unkindly. "I don't want to be here all night."

Zoey put her hands on her hips. "We are out here in the cold and the dark helping you when you were vandalizing our property. You need to apologize if you want us to help you."

The boy pressed his lips together and looked aside.

Timothy took Zoey's arm and led her away. "Come on, let's go."

"Wait!" called the boy. "You'd better come back!"

As the two headed home, they had to move slowly. It was so dark, and the beams from the flashlights didn't light up much of the surrounding area. Timothy also noted that it was getting foggy. His hands and nose stung from the cold air.

Just as they were stepping over a large log, an unexpected, stern female voice rang through the trees and made them both halt abruptly.

"Stop right there!"

Whirling around, Timothy and Zoey found themselves blinded by the light of a flashlight pointed directly at them.

"Are you Zoey and Timothy?" the voice asked.

Timothy gulped and answered weakly, "Yes."

The light lowered to the ground and Timothy could see that the voice belonged to a police officer.

"Your parents were worried about you. They came home to find the front door wide open, and you were gone. We were about to start a search party to look for you."

"We left my mom's phone out here and came to get it," Zoey said, holding up the phone.

"Well, let's get you back now," the woman said and radioed to another police officer that the children had been found.

Zoey spoke up. "But there is a boy who needs our help. He was vandalizing our property and got tangled in a bush as he tried to run away."

The woman shook her head. "What a night! Take me to him. I'll make sure your parents know you are OK." She radioed more information to the other police officer, and by the time they got to the boy, three other police officers had joined them. Two of them insisted on taking Zoey and Timothy home. The other two stayed and started helping the boy get untangled.

"What will happen to him?" Zoey asked a police officer before they left.

"He was trespassing. He'll be arrested."

CHAPTER 10

T IMOTHY TOSSED AND TURNED MUCH OF the night, but he finally fell into a deep sleep and woke up later than normal.

Nanna Rose and Papa George were setting their suitcases by the door.

"I wish we didn't have to leave," Papa George declared. "Things are pretty exciting around here!"

"And we will miss you all so much," Nanna Rose added.

"You'll come again soon, won't you?" Zoey asked.

Papa George winked at her. "You'd better believe it. And I'm happy to throw pine cones at intruders next time I come too!"

After sending Nanna Rose and Papa George off with lots of hugs, the family sat together and discussed the night before.

"Now that we've had some time to think about what happened and settle down from the fright, we should talk about last night," John began. "You two knew that you shouldn't have left the house at night."

Lily cut in, "Imagine how afraid we were when we found the house empty and the front door wide open. You should have called to let us know what was going on."

The children nodded their heads, understanding.

"We would have, Mom, but our phone watches were dead, and I was afraid it would get too dark if we waited to charge them," Zoey said softly.

"You two will need to do an hour of extra chores each day for the next two weeks," John said.

Timothy nodded slowly. "That's fair. We are really sorry."

"Yes, we are very, really, truly, definitely sorry," Zoey added. "I didn't want you to think less of me for leaving your phone outside, and I didn't want it to get ruined."

"I know," Lily said softly. "We just hope you will think more clearly next time. My phone can be replaced. Your safety is what matters most."

The children both nodded.

John stood up. "Lily and I will make a chart with extra things that need to be done around the house and yard. Each day, set a timer and do sixty minutes of things on the chart. OK?"

The children nodded again.

Lily stood up too. "We'll let you two get started on school and chores. John and I are going to head down to the police station to talk to Andrew, the boy who got stuck in the bush while trespassing on our farm."

"What will happen to him?" Timothy asked, feeling glad that Andrew had gotten caught but also sad that he was in trouble.

"Trespassing and vandalizing can have some serious penalties," John explained. "Lily

102

and I prayed last night and this morning for direction on what to do. We'll let you know how it goes."

"Make sure to focus and do your schoolwork carefully," Lily added as she walked to the front door. "We'll do history over lunch, and then Mrs. Bastian is coming over a little later."

After their parents shut the front door, Timothy turned to Zoey. "I forgot Mrs. Bastian was coming. I can't wait!"

"Me either," Zoey agreed. "But I do feel bad about causing Mom and Dad stress. I have an idea. What if we really focus and do our schoolwork quickly and then clean up the whole house? We could even make lunch for Mom and Dad and make them each cards to tell them how sorry we are."

"Well, OK," Timothy agreed.

He had to admit that the challenge was actually fun. They carefully completed their schoolwork and then wrote cards for their parents. Afterward, they ran around like a whirlwind, cleaning up the house and making lunch.

John and Lily were pleasantly surprised when they came home. They were also happy with the way things had turned out at the police station.

"We talked kindly to the boy," Lily said. "We explained to him how special Badger Hills Farm is and how we protect and care for it. We talked for a long time, actually. Then we decided that we would drop the charges."

"It felt right," John added. "After we told

him that we were dropping charges, he told us that he was going to talk to his friends and make sure they never come on our land again."

"That's great!" Zoey cried.

"Yes," Timothy said, "but I'd still feel safer if we had a fence around this place."

"Me too!" John and Lily said at the same time.

After lunch, Mrs. Bastian arrived. Everyone chatted for a while before Lily got the letter tiles they had been using to figure out the message on the stamps.

"I need the actual stamps," Mrs. Bastian said, wheeling up to the table in front of the fireplace. She took the Bible that was in her lap and plunked it on the table.

Timothy felt his heart beating faster. *This is*

exciting. What does Mrs. Bastian know?

John went and got the box where they had put the stamps after they had taken them out of the book. He offered the box to Mrs. Bastian, along with the tweezers they had used.

First, Mrs. Bastian opened the Bible to the first page.

"What do you see written?" she asked Zoey.

Zoey studied the handwritten text. "Birth years of the Roach family members."

"That's right," Mrs. Bastian said. "And Timothy, are the dates in any kind of order?"

"They are in chronological order by the year each person was born."

"That's right," Mrs. Bastian declared again. "I believe if we put these stamps in chronological order, it could reveal the correct message."

"Brilliant!" John exclaimed. "Let's try it."

Mrs. Bastian picked up each stamp with the tweezers and showed the back of each to Lily. Lily then matched a letter tile with the stamp. Then the stamp was laid down on the table. The group kept moving the stamps with their associated letter tiles to put them in chronological order by the year each stamp was issued.

Timothy pressed his hands together in excitement as he realized that it seemed to be working. So far, putting the stamps in chronological order by year had revealed three real words that made sense together:

The rarest stamp

"It's making a sentence!" Zoey cried. "It's working!"

Everyone was gathered around the table.

Mrs. Bastian laughed. "This is better than any adventure I've written about in my books!"

More words were formed as they placed the stamps in order. Timothy now read more of the sentence:

The rarest stamp is in the

"There are only four more stamps to go!" John said.

That made Timothy's heart drop as he suddenly remembered the two stamps that had flown into the fireplace. What if those two stamps had letters on them?

As they continued putting the stamps in

order, it became obvious that the burned stamps were needed because there were two letters missing in the middle of the last word. The group looked at the sentence.

The rarest stamp is in the sco__e

Everyone was quiet. They had gotten so close! But no one knew what the last word could be, and no one wanted to make Timothy feel bad by bringing up the missing letters.

Then Lily cocked her head before turning to Timothy. "Oh! I know what the word is! Timothy, our history lesson . . . the one we just had during lunch . . . what was it on?"

"Medieval castles."

"Yes, and we learned the name of the item that they put on castle walls to hold candles or torches. What was it called?"

"A sconce," Timothy replied.

"And where in this house is a sconce?"

Timothy wrinkled his forehead. Then his eyes suddenly widened. "The hidden room."

CHAPTER 11

LILY HELD UP A LANTERN AS JOHN removed the sconces from the wall of the hidden room.

"Are you sure all the electricity to this room has been turned off?" Lily asked with concern.

"I'm positive," John reassured her. "I triple-checked that the breakers were off before we came down here."

John gave another firm tug, and the second sconce popped away from the wall with a rattle.

"There," John said. "Let's get these upstairs and take a closer look."

John and Lily brought the sconces into the family room, where everyone waited. They carefully placed them on the table.

Zoey and Timothy leaned over one of the sconces and began inspecting it closely. They pushed and pulled and took apart anything that was removable.

"Oh!" Zoey said suddenly. "Look! This part of the sconce comes out. It's a little box!"

Everyone leaned in to get a closer look at the small wooden box. Zoey started to open the top but then hesitated. She handed the box to Timothy.

"I found the box, so Timothy can open it," Zoey said with a smile.

"Thank you," Timothy replied, carefully taking the box from Zoey.

The room held its breath as Timothy opened the tiny box with squeaky hinges. Inside, one small stamp lay by itself atop dark red velvet.

"Wow," Timothy breathed. "It looks so important."

"It's hard to see what's on the stamp," Lily said. "Can you tell, Timothy?"

Timothy squinted at the box. "It looks like a group of people and maybe a table."

Zoey dashed off and came back with the stamp tweezers and magnifying glass. "Maybe these will help," she said.

Timothy put the box on the table and carefully picked the stamp up with the tweezers. Then he positioned the magnifying glass over the stamp.

John gasped as the image became clear. "That's the signing of the Declaration of Independence, but why is it upside down?"

"The Inverted Jenny was worth so much money," Zoey reminded everyone. "Maybe this one is too!"

Lily pulled out her phone, typed for a few seconds, and then gasped. Her eyes widened. "If this is what I think it is . . ." Her voice trailed off as she started tapping on the phone screen again. "I'm calling Mr. Garcia," she said as she walked into the kitchen.

Timothy carefully placed the stamp back on the red velvet inside the box.

"It sounds like the stamp might be really important," John said.

Lily came back into the room, a huge smile on her face. "Mr. Garcia is on his way over. He was so excited that he didn't even say goodbye before he hung up!"

Lily researched the stamp a little more while they waited for Mr. Garcia to arrive.

"I think this might be an unused Declaration of Independence stamp from 1869. If so, only four other unused copies are known to exist in the world today!" Lily shared.

"Wow," John declared. "It must be worth a fortune."

A knock at the door interrupted everyone's thoughts. John rushed to the door and opened it. Mr. Garcia stood on the porch looking both excited and anxious.

"May I see it?" he blurted and then turned

a little red. "Oh, my apologies. Where are my manners? Hello, John, so nice to see you again."

John smiled and motioned Mr. Garcia inside. "No need to apologize. We are all excited to learn more about this stamp. Please, come inside."

Timothy got up from his chair and offered it to Mr. Garcia as he came into the family room.

"This is so exciting," Mr. Garcia said as he rolled out a little case of special stamp tools on the table. He selected a small pair of stamp tongs and a magnifier lens that he held to his eye by squinting. He leaned over the box and very slowly and carefully lifted the stamp out with the tongs to get a better look.

After studying it for a minute, he placed it

back in the box, closed the lid, and replaced his tools in the case.

Everyone watched him expectantly.

"It is definitely an inverted Declaration of Independence stamp that was printed in 1869," Mr. Garcia said at last.

Lily gasped and put her hand over her mouth to stifle an excited squeal. Having just researched the stamp on the internet, she appeared to have a pretty good idea of what Mr. Garcia was about to say.

"It is my opinion, after carefully observing the stamp's condition," Mr. Garcia began, "that it would easily sell at auction for at least 1.5 million dollars."

His words lingered in the stunned silence of the room.

"Are you serious?" John asked at last.

"Oh, quite serious," Mr. Garcia replied with a smile. "And there's an auction next month that I could enter it in."

John looked at Lily, who was beaming. "God has provided a way to complete the improvements we've dreamed about," she said.

"Wahoo!" Timothy yelled.

"Banana burrito humongous mosquito!" Zoey exclaimed. "That is incredible!"

John grinned. "It sure is. We can put up that beautiful fence!"

☙

Mr. Garcia registered the stamp at the auction the next month, where it sold for just over 1.6 million dollars. It was enough money to put up the perimeter fence and the fence around the future campground as well.

The whole family gathered on a hill to watch the big tractors knock down the old wall to make way for the new stone wall with the wrought iron fence on top.

"Isn't it great that Badger Hills Farm will be safe with this beautiful fence?" Timothy said to Zoey.

"Yeah. I still can't believe that little stamp was worth so much money," she replied.

Timothy nodded and looked around at his family.

It's fun to search for all these treasures, he thought, *but the truth is, my family is the greatest treasure I could have.*

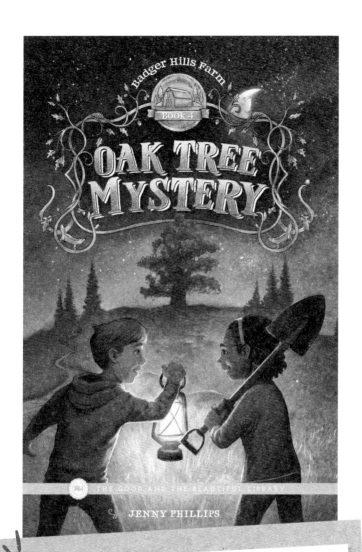

Continue the adventures of Timothy and Zoey with *Oak Tree Mystery*—Book 4 of the Badger Hills Farm series by Jenny Phillips.

Available at
goodandbeautiful.com

MORE BOOKS FROM
THE GOOD AND THE BEAUTIFUL

Prince Percy and the
Big Red Ruby
By Jenny Phillips

Helen Keller:
Into the Light
By Shannen Yauger

GOODANDBEAUTIFUL.COM